D1611208

4191

Main str.

12.90

A Discovery Biography

Eli Whitney

— ◆ —

Great Inventor

by Jean Lee Latham
illustrated by Cary

CHELSEA JUNIORS
A division of Chelsea House Publishers
New York ◆ Philadelphia

The Discovery Biographies have been prepared under the
educational supervision of Mary C. Austin, Ed.D.,
Reading Specialist and Professor of Education, Case
Western Reserve University.

Cover illustration: Viqui Maggio

First Chelsea House edition 1991

1   3   5   7   9   8   6   4   2

ISBN   0-7910-1453-3

Contents

Eli Whitney:
Great Inventor

Chapter *1*

Almost a Man

Eli awakened early on December 8, 1775. "Eli Whitney," he told himself, "you are ten today, almost a man."

Besides being almost a man, he was the oldest child. Elizabeth was eight, Benjamin was six, and little Josiah was five.

"You must help Papa more with the farm," Eli said to himself. "Times are hard."

Times are hard. Everybody said that.

America was at war with England. The American Revolution had started last April. Every day Eli saw men going toward Boston, thirty miles away. They had to leave their farms and shops to join the army. So food was scarce and prices were high.

"You must be more help," Eli said again. He dressed and hurried out to the barn.

"You're up early," Papa said. He smiled for a minute. Then the smile went away.

Eli could remember when Papa had laughed a lot. That was before Mama had gotten sick. For five long years she had lain in her bed.

"I'm almost a man," Eli said. "I'm going to be more help."

All day Friday and Saturday he worked hard. Sunday morning he helped Elizabeth dress their little brothers for church. He wrapped hot bricks in pieces of blanket and carried them out to the sleigh.

Then he went to Mama's room to say good-by. How pale and thin she was! Eli could remember when she had laughed a lot, too. He could remember when she sang as she worked.

He started to tiptoe from the room. He stopped. Papa had forgotten his watch. Eli stood looking at it. If only he could take that watch apart!

Eli went out to the sleigh. He put his hands over his stomach. He screwed up his face. "I don't feel good," he said. "I'd better stay home."

He watched the sleigh drive away. He went back into the house. He tiptoed to Mama's room and got the watch.

The next thing Eli heard was the sound of hoofbeats. He jumped. He stared down at the pieces of the watch spread out on the table. Was church over? Was Papa back already? No, the hoofbeats did not stop.

He shut his eyes a minute to remember how the watch had looked. He put it back together. Soon he had it running. He set it to the right time by the tall clock in the corner. He tiptoed to Mama's room.

She was awake. "Eli, dear, what is wrong? Why aren't you at church?"

He knelt by her bed. He told her what he had done.

"I know I've been bad," he said. "But I just *had* to see what was inside that watch!"

"Oh, Eli!" She covered her face with her hands. Her shoulders shook.

"Mama, I'm sorry! Please don't cry!"

"I'm laughing." And she was! "Is the watch running all right?"

"Of course. I put it back together just the way it was."

"I'm proud of you. But, Eli . . ."

"Yes, Mama?"

"I think this had better be our own little joke. I don't believe anybody else would think it was funny." She smiled. "I remember when you were just a little fellow . . ."

When the others came from church Mama was still talking. She was telling Eli about the things he tried to take apart when he was little.

Papa smiled, too. "You're looking better!" he told her.

"I feel better," she said. "I'll be up and around soon."

But she was not "up and around soon." Two summers later, when Eli was eleven, she died.

Chapter 2

Not Much of a Farmer

It was not Sunday, but Eli was dressing his brothers in their Sunday best. He combed Benjamin's hair and looked at Josiah's ears.

"Now, stand up straight," he said, "and mind what I tell you."

Elizabeth smiled. "They'll mind you, Eli. They look up to you. We all have to *look up* to you."

Eli grinned. That was their joke. He was thirteen now and growing very tall. He turned to his brothers.

15

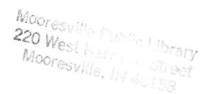

"We are going to have a new mama and two new sisters. Hannah is eleven. Nancy is younger. We must be polite and make them feel at home."

"Yes, Eli!" they promised.

It was almost suppertime when they heard the horses stop.

"Come on!" Eli said. He marched them out to say hello to their new mama and sisters. Then he helped Papa carry in a lot of boxes.

His stepmother snatched one small, flat box from his hands. "Don't drop that!" She opened the box. It had a set of knives in it.

"I wasn't going to drop that box," Eli thought. But he did not say it. Instead, he tried to think of something nice to say to his new stepmother.

16

"I could make a knife like those if I had the tools. I could even make the tools to make the knife with, if I had the tools to make the tools with."

Papa smiled and started to say something.

But Eli's stepmother sniffed. "Oh, is that so? You could make a knife like these? Hah!"

Hannah, the older sister, giggled shrilly.

Papa stopped smiling. He said quietly, "Eli is not much of a farmer. But he is handy with tools."

The new mama sniffed again. "It would take more than a handy man to make one of these knives!"

"I wonder if she ever smiles?" Eli thought.

18

Chapter *3*

No Future for a Handy Man

A few months later one of the knives got broken. Eli made a new blade for it, exactly like the others. He took it in the house to his stepmother.

"Well!" She sounded surprised. She still did not smile.

Eli went back out to Papa's workshop in the barn. He did not stay in the house very much.

"Papa, I have an idea." Eli was almost fifteen now and as tall as his father.

"Yes, son?"

Eli laid two handmade nails on the workbench. "If we had a forge to heat the iron, I could make nails. They are very scarce now. People would pay good money for them."

"It takes more than a forge to make nails, Eli. It takes a lot of know-how. The man who made those nails had to spend a long time . . . What are you laughing at?"

"I made them myself, down at the blacksmith shop."

"Eli! You're not much of a farmer, but you certainly are a handy man. You are a very *handy* handy man!"

Soon Eli had his forge. He sold all the nails he made. He whistled as he worked. He was happier than he had been for a long time.

In 1783 the war ended. Everybody but Eli celebrated. Eli was too busy making nails. A Mr. Robert Smith had given him a big order.

One day Mr. Smith came into the shop. "I won't want those nails, Eli."

"What? But why not, Mr. Smith?"

"I have just been to Boston. We can get nails from England again. They are cheaper. Your little handy-man business was all right during the war. But there is no future for a handy man now."

Chapter *4*

A Waste of a Good Mechanic

No future for a handy man. Eli remembered those words many times in the next two years.

One night at the supper table he said, "Papa, there is no future for a handy man. I want to make something of my life. I want to go to college."

Hannah giggled the way she always did. "You go to college! I've heard you were always the slowest reader in your class!"

Eli's stepmother frowned. "College! The very idea! Do you know what it would cost to send you to college for four years? At least a thousand dollars! Your father isn't going to take the bread out of our mouths to make a fine gentleman of you!"

Hannah giggled again. "Don't worry. It would take him ten years just to get ready for college."

"I know it will take me a while," Eli said. "Maybe when I am ready money won't be so scarce. I'll pay my own way while I'm getting ready."

"How?" Papa asked.

"I got a job over at Grafton today. I'll get my room and meals and seven dollars a month. I am going to teach school."

Papa stared. "You got the job?"

"Yes, sir."

"Do they know how dumb you are?" Hannah asked.

"Yes, Hannah," Eli said quietly. "I told them that I was not a very quick student. And do you know what one man said? He said that sometimes a slow learner made a good teacher. He has more patience. I think I'll do all right, if I work hard enough."

He did work hard. In the winter he taught school. Before dawn he tramped to the one-room school. He started a fire in the fireplace. Then he sat down, still bundled up in his overcoat. He planned the lessons for his students.

In the summer he went to Leicester Academy. He worked even harder there.

He was up at four o'clock studying. He studied at night until he fell asleep over his Greek and Latin books. His stepmother sniffed at the idea. "What good is Greek and Latin to you? You'll never be more than a handy man!"

"I am paying my own way," was all Eli ever said.

He did try to tell his father how he felt. "You know how muscles grow strong from using, Papa? Well, I can feel the muscles in my brain growing strong from using, too."

"You are driving yourself mighty hard," Papa said. "How long can you keep it up?"

"Until I am ready for Yale."

"I don't know where the money is coming from," Papa said.

The spring of 1789 Eli told his family he was going to Yale.

"What about money?" Papa asked.

"I have enough money to get to New Haven," Eli said. "I can get a job. I can work part time and go to Yale part time."

His father drove him to Brookfield to catch the stagecoach for New Haven. "The neighbors think it is very silly for you to go to college, Eli. They say it is a waste of a good mechanic."

"I know. I have heard them talking."

Papa said no more. In Brookfield he watched the stagecoach drive up. He said good-by. Then suddenly he pulled out his purse. "Here, Eli. This is all the money I can give you now. I'll send you a little more whenever I can.

You'll get that thousand dollars. I don't know how, but you'll get it."

"Thank you, Papa! I'll pay back every penny when I get out of Yale."

"You aren't even *in* Yale yet, Eli," Papa said. "I hear President Stiles will ask you questions all day. Then maybe he will say you aren't ready for Yale. I—I hope you do get in, Eli." He did not sound very hopeful.

Chapter *5*

A Late Start

Eli sat in front of President Stiles and tried to keep his hands from shaking.

"How old are you, Mr. Whitney?"

"Twenty-three, sir."

President Stiles said nothing. Eli knew what he must be thinking. *A late start.* It was a late start. Eli knew that. He had seen how young the boys were. Some were fourteen or fifteen. One boy was only eleven.

The questions began. They went on hour after hour.

At last the president stopped. "You know the school year is half over, don't you?"

"Yes, sir."

"It would be easier for you to wait and enter in the fall."

Eli's heart sank.

Then the president smiled. "But I do not believe you are looking for what is 'easier,' Mr. Whitney. You may enter Yale now." He got up. "I am going over to our museum. Come along. I think it may interest you."

Eli followed. He was too tired to pay much attention to anything. Then he came to a table full of machinery.

"We use these in some of our lectures," the president said.

"Is it all right to touch them?"

32

The president nodded. Presently he said, "Mr. Whitney . . . "

Eli jumped. How long had he been standing there?

The president's eyes twinkled. "Do you know what I'll do if your seat is ever empty in a class? I'll tell them to look for you here."

Eli grinned. But he thought, "My seat empty in a class? Never! I would not miss hearing one of his lectures for anything! I'll drink up college like a dry field drinks up rain!"

One day in his second year Eli was almost late to a class. A new machine had just come from England. It was called an *orrery*. It was a set of little balls that ran by clockwork.

The middle ball was supposed to be the sun. The other balls were the planets. They moved around the sun, keeping perfect time.

Eli could hardly tear himself away from the orrery. He ran to class and got there panting. President Stiles gave him a long, quiet stare.

Not long afterwards a student knocked over the orrery and broke it. "I'll pay to have it fixed, sir!" he promised. "Right away!"

"It cannot be fixed 'right away,' " the president said. "We shall have to send it back to England to be fixed."

Eli's only free hour all day was just after the noon meal. The next day at one o'clock he went to the museum. He carefully took the broken orrery apart.

Finally he put it back together. He wound it. It ran perfectly.

Behind Eli the president spoke. "I thought I might find you here."

Eli jumped. He looked toward the windows. It was late! He had missed his afternoon classes!

President Stiles was not frowning. He was looking at the orrery. "What are you going to do after college, Mr. Whitney?"

"Get ready to be a lawyer, sir."

"A lawyer?"

"There is no future in America for a handy man, sir."

"Do you know how long it will take you?" the president asked. "You will have to read law, night and day, for at least two years."

"It will take me longer than that, sir," Eli said. "I shall have to earn my living, too. I shall probably teach by day and read law by night."

President Stiles said nothing. He was looking at the orrery.

Chapter *6*

"It Can't Be Done!"

The fall of 1792 Eli was graduated from Yale. He was almost twenty-seven. It had been a long row to hoe. How much longer, he wondered, before he would be a lawyer? Well, at least he had a job.

President Stiles had told him about a job in the South. "A man asked Phineas Miller to find him a teacher for his children. Phineas used to be a student here. He came to me. I told him about you."

"Thank you, sir."

"You may like the South," said the president. "Mr. Miller went there to teach. Now he manages a big plantation named Mulberry Grove."

"I think I've heard of Mulberry Grove," Eli said. "Isn't it the farm that Georgia gave to General Nathanael Greene after the war?"

The president smiled. "It's hardly a farm, Mr. Whitney. It is probably bigger than two dozen New England farms. It is almost like a little village. Poor General Greene did not have long to enjoy it. He died in 1786. He owed thousands of dollars. He had borrowed money to feed his starving soldiers. He was a fine, brave man. His widow is a fine woman.

It was not easy for her to be left a widow with five little children. You will enjoy the trip south with Mr. Miller, Mrs. Greene and her family."

Eli went to New York City to meet Mrs. Greene. What a surprise she was! He had expected to see somebody pale and sad and brave. Mrs. Greene was beautiful and gay.

"How nice that you can make the trip south with us, Mr. Whitney!" she said. "You must pay us a nice long visit at Mulberry Grove before you start teaching."

Eli could only stare at her. Was she asking a perfect stranger to "pay a nice long visit?"

She was. He did stop at Mulberry Grove. But he had more surprises.

President Stiles had said Mrs. Greene was in debt. But gay visitors came and went in the big, beautiful house.

Nobody seemed to worry. Eli tried to think of ways to help Mrs. Greene. He mended toys for the children. He made her a new set of embroidery hoops.

"Mr. Whitney," she said, "you are a mechanical genius!"

"Just a handy man," he told her.

That night three plantation owners came to visit.

"We've got to find something we can grow and sell," Major Bremen said. "If we don't, we'll be ruined."

"We could grow upland cotton," another said.

"It's no use," Major Bremen said. "No cotton gin can seed it."

"What's a cotton gin?" Eli asked.

"*Gin* is short for *engine*," Major Bremen told him. "A cotton gin takes the seeds out of cotton. But no cotton gin can seed upland cotton. A man has to seed it by hand. It takes him a whole day to seed one pound. If only we had a gin that would seed it! That would be a great thing for the South!"

"Ask Mr. Whitney to invent one," Mrs. Greene said. "He is a mechanical genius. Look at the beautiful embroidery hoops he made for me!"

Major Bremen smiled. "Men have tried for hundreds of years to invent a gin to seed upland cotton. It can't be done."

Chapter 7

Bad News

The next day Eli found some upland cotton. It looked like a fluffy ball. He pulled the ball open. Inside he found fuzzy green seeds. The cotton stuck to the fuzz. He had to pull hard to get it off.

"We need to *pull off* the cotton lint and to *hold back* the seeds," Eli said. "But how?" He began to think.

After ten days he told Phineas, "I believe I can build a gin to seed upland cotton."

"Then you have a partner!" Phineas said. "I'll pay all the expenses!"

Eli gave up the thought of teaching. He gave up the thought of reading law. He shut himself up in a room and worked. Nobody but Phineas and Mrs. Greene saw what he was doing.

But people did ask questions. What was going on at Mulberry Grove? Why did Phineas Miller keep buying upland cotton?

After six months Eli said, "There! I have solved the last problem! My gin can seed fifty pounds of upland cotton in one day!"

Little Cornelia Greene begged to see the gin.

"You may see it if you promise not to talk about it," Phineas told her.

"We must keep it a secret until Mr. Whitney gets a patent."

"What is a patent?" she asked.

"A patent is something to save great inventions for the world," Phineas said. "This is the way it works. The inventor must write down how he makes his machine and how it works. He must build a little copy of the machine and give it to the government. Then, if he should die, his invention will not be lost. Other men will know how to make it."

"What if the inventor doesn't die?" she asked.

"He gets a patent on his invention. Nobody can copy his machine while the patent lasts. They call that 'the life of the patent.' It lasts fourteen years."

Cornelia promised she would keep the secret. Eli showed her the cotton gin.

It was a box with a curved shelf in the middle. The shelf was made of iron with narrow slits in it. There was a handle on the side of the box. Eli turned the handle. Little wire teeth came up through the slits in the shelf.

Eli piled some cotton on the shelf. He turned the handle again. The wire teeth pulled the cotton off the seeds. The cotton went through the narrow slits. But the seeds were too big to go through the slits. Eli had found the way to "pull off the cotton and hold back the seeds."

He raised the shelf. Cornelia could see two wooden rollers inside the box.

One roller had rows of wire teeth. The other roller had brushes.

"The roller with brushes takes the cotton lint off the wires," Eli said. "Do you understand?"

"Oh, yes! It's very simple, isn't it? Almost anybody could make one, after you thought up how."

"That's why we must keep it a secret."

"How long?" Cornelia asked.

"Until I go to Philadelphia and get a patent. Philadelphia is the capital of our country. That is where the Patent Office is."

"You'll hurry back, won't you?" she begged.

"I'm afraid not, Cornelia. I must stay up north to build cotton gins. I shall make the gins in New Haven.

I can get the things I'll need to work with easier up there."

"But you *will* come back someday, won't you?"

"Of course he will!" Phineas promised. "He'll probably come in a golden coach! He's going to be a very rich man!"

Eli and Phineas became partners. Phineas gave Eli the money he needed to get started.

"After the first year," Phineas said, "we won't have to worry about money."

Eli smiled when he said good-by. "I may not write often."

"I'll not worry!" Phineas said. "Nothing can go wrong!"

But things did go wrong. There was a very bad outbreak of yellow fever.

People were dying by dozens in New Haven. Eli could not get workmen to start building his cotton gins. Yellow fever was even worse in Philadelphia. People were dying by hundreds there. Weeks passed. Eli still did not have the patent on his cotton gin.

Things went wrong in Mulberry Grove, too. Phineas wrote the bad news. Someone had broken in and had stolen the cotton gin.

Eli thought of what Cornelia had said. *"Almost anybody could make one, after you thought up how."*

Chapter **8**

Worse News

Next spring, Phineas put a notice in a Georgia paper. Eli shook his head as he read it. Phineas promised he would be ready to seed upland cotton that fall. He would be ready to seed all the upland cotton Georgia raised. He would have cotton gins at handy places all over the state.

Eli looked at a map of Georgia. He thought of the bad roads. Two hundred gins would not be enough to cover the state. Eli knew he could not build half that many gins by fall.

He shook his head over the rest of the notice, too. What about the way Phineas was going to charge for seeding the cotton? The notice said that the planters would get back "one pound of clean lint for every five pounds of cotton." Eli knew that five pounds of cotton would make almost two pounds of clean lint. Phineas was going to keep almost half the cotton he seeded. What would the planters think of that? Would they think Miller and Whitney were charging too much for seeding their cotton?

"Well," Eli thought, "Phineas lives in Georgia. He ought to know what he's doing. I hope he isn't making a mistake."

But by the spring of 1798 they knew Phineas had made a mistake. The high price he charged for seeding the cotton had made the planters angry. And Eli could not build enough gins to keep up with the cotton crop. There were not Miller-Whitney gins "at handy places all over the state." Planters had to take their cotton long miles over bad roads to reach a Miller-Whitney gin.

Now there were hundreds of copies of the cotton gin all over the state. Phineas was bringing lawsuits against the men who made them. But the courts were siding with the planters. The judges said these gins were not copies.

Miller and Whitney had not won a single case.

There was worse trouble, too. The planters had spread a story that Eli's cotton gin ruined the lint. So his gins were standing idle.

A new day had dawned for Georgia. Planters were getting rich on upland cotton. Ship owners were getting rich carrying millions of pounds of cotton to England. But Eli was in debt.

What could he do? It was no use to build more cotton gins. Eli tried to sleep and could not. He tried to read and could not keep his mind on the words.

One day, though, something in a newspaper did catch his eye. There was a great deal of talk about war.

America and France were having trouble. America was building warships. Congress had voted to spend $800,000 for guns and cannons. The government wanted to buy at least 40,000 muskets.

"From where?" Eli thought. "It takes a lifetime to train a good gun-smith. There aren't enough gunsmiths in America to make forty *dozen* muskets!"

Suddenly he laid down the paper. He began to think. He remembered how he had helped his men build cotton gins. He thought of some of the tools he had made to help them. If he could make tools to help make the pieces of a musket . . .

He began to plan. He wrote to Oliver Wolcott, Secretary of the Treasury.

He promised that he could build 10,000 muskets for the government.

A letter called him to Philadelphia right away. Soon Eli was back in New Haven with a contract for $134,000! He was to build 10,000 muskets for the government at $13.40 each.

Mr. Wolcott had given him $5,000 to help him get started. His hard times were over!

Chapter *9*

The Worst News of All

His hard times were over! That was what Eli thought.

But there was another outbreak of yellow fever in Philadelphia. All business came to a standstill. Eli had expected to get iron and gun barrels there. He could get nothing.

In New Haven he tried to buy the land he wanted for his factory. It was an old mill by a river dam. He would need water power to run his machinery. He tried to buy the land in June. It was September before he got it.

He knew he must build his factory very quickly. He must have the roof on the building before the first snowfall. It was a race against time. Eli lost the race. The first snowfall came early. More snowstorms came, one after the other, all winter.

The next February Eli's work was at a standstill. He had not gotten a single pound of iron. He could not make a single tool for his workmen. He had run out of money.

He wrote to Mr. Wolcott. The Secretary of the Treasury was very understanding. He sent more money.

At last Eli could get iron. He began to make tools. He began to train his men. But summer came and passed. In September he had not made one musket.

He had promised 4,000 muskets by then.

At last his factory was in operation. Men came to see the work. But they went away puzzled. Where were the muskets? The workers were not making muskets. They were just making odd-shaped little pieces.

By September of 1800 Eli still had not made one musket. He had promised 10,000 muskets by then. He wrote again to explain to Mr. Wolcott.

In December Eli got a letter from Washington, the new capital of the United States. Mr. Wolcott was no longer Secretary of the Treasury. The new Secretary had been looking over the records. The government had sent a great deal of money to Mr. Whitney. Where were the muskets?

Eli knew that was his darkest hour. He knew the government might take the contract away from him. Then he would have to give back all the money Mr. Wolcott had sent him.

"If I lose the contract," Eli thought, "I am ruined!"

Chapter *10*

One Last Chance

Eli went to Washington to explain about the muskets. He knew it was his last chance. Several stern-faced men waited for him.

"Do you have the muskets?" an army officer asked.

"No," Eli said, "but I have something better." He opened several boxes and set them on the table.

"What is 'better' than the muskets you promised?'

Eli did not answer that. He said, "You know it takes a lifetime to train a gunsmith. His hardest job is to make the musket lock. He must file and polish each part until it will fit. Then what does he have? He has a part that will fit one musket but no other."

"Of course," the officer said.

"My workmen are not gunsmiths," Eli said. "So I have made patterns and tools to guide their hands. A man makes just one part of the lock. But that part is perfect. It is exactly like all the others he makes. It will fit any of my musket locks. I call that mass production."

"But that is impossible!"

Eli pointed to the boxes. "There are the pieces of fifty musket locks. Suppose you take a piece from each box. Put a lock together."

"It's impossible!" the officer said again. But he took a piece from each box. He put the lock together. He jumped to his feet. "Sir, you've done it! This is the greatest invention in the world!"

Eli smiled. He thought of his years of work. Now he knew he had won. "Maybe," he said, "there *is* a future in America for a handy man."

"Sir, you are no handy man! You are a mechanical genius!"

Eli laughed. "Do you know what a mechanical genius is? He is a handy man who succeeds."

70

This time Eli knew his troubles were over. The government believed in him. He would have the time and the money he needed to finish his muskets. Now he had nothing to do but make muskets by mass production.

"Of course I'll work from dawn to dark," he thought. "My men need me right there with them every minute. But I'll be there!" He hurried back to his factory.

A letter from Phineas waited for him in New Haven. "Good news! Get ready to build cotton gins again! I think we will get a contract with the state of South Carolina! I am busy with these court cases here in Georgia. So you will have to see about things in South Carolina."

Month after month, year after year, Eli tried to do three jobs. He made muskets. He built cotton gins. He traveled back and forth to the South.

By the winter of 1803 he knew he could not go on that way. He wrote to Phineas. "You will have to take care of everything in the South. I must stay in New Haven. No man can do three jobs."

Just as Eli finished writing, one of his men came in. "A letter for you, Mr. Whitney. From Georgia."

Eli opened the letter. He read it. Slowly he tore up his letter to Phineas. It was no use to send it now. Phineas was dead.

Chapter *11*

No Man Can Do
Three Jobs

"No man can do three jobs," Eli thought, "but I am going to have to!"

And he did. He helped his men make muskets. Then something would go wrong with the cotton gin. He helped those men. Then something would go wrong with the muskets.

Then he would have to make another long trip south. While he was away, things would go wrong with cotton gins and muskets, both.

He won a contract with South Carolina. That state said the cotton gin was his invention. All the other gins were imitations of his. South Carolina paid him $50,000 for the use of his gin in that state.

North Carolina and Tennessee soon followed South Carolina. There, too, men said the gin was his invention.

At last, after sixty court cases, Eli won in Georgia. A judge said "Eli Whitney is the inventor of the cotton gin. All other gins are copies of his. The cotton gin belongs to him for the life of the patent!"

For the life of the patent. But it had taken him over thirteen years to win. It was now May, 1807. The life of the patent would end in November.

And that would be the end of any chance to make money on his patent.

Eli went back to work on the muskets. In January, 1809, he delivered the last of the 10,000. It had taken him ten years instead of two.

A contract for $134,000! Life would be easier now. Of course, the government had sent him money from time to time. How much of the $134,000 was left? Eli opened his record book. He added the columns of figures. He laid down his pen. He sat a long time with his head in his hands. He would get less than $2,500.

Years later Eli could look back on his long, hard struggle with a smile.

He was rich and world famous. And he was not alone now. He had a wife and two little girls. Then their third child was born—a boy.

Eli was beaming as he walked to the factory. "I hope," he thought, "that my men are as happy as I am!"

Two of his men were yelling at each other. They saw him coming and stopped shouting.

"What's wrong?" Eli asked.

"We were just having a friendly little talk," the first man said.

"Friendly?"

The man grinned. "We want to get a present for Eli, Junior. We were talking about what we'd write on the card. I wanted, 'May you invent something as great as the cotton gin.'"

The second man said, "And I wanted, 'May you invent something as great as mass production.'"

"I say the cotton gin is the greatest invention in the world!" the first man shouted. "Look what it's done for America! We grow more cotton than any other country! We—"

The second man shouted, "And I say mass production is greater than the cotton gin! Look what it's going to mean to everybody! Things made by hand cost a lot. Only rich men can buy them. Things made by mass production will be cheaper. Even people like us can buy them! I say—" He stopped yelling and grinned. "*You* settle it, Mr. Whitney. What do you want us to write?"

"I don't know what he'll be when he grows up," Eli said. "He may be a doctor, a lawyer or a minister. He may be a handy man. But, whatever he is, there will be a future for him in America. So how about—"

"I've got it!" the first man said. " 'To Eli Whitney, Junior. America will have a place for you. And your father helped to make it!' "